Free Verse Editions

Edited by Jon Thompson

Also by Daniel Tiffany

Poetry

The Work-Shy (under the signature of Blunt Research Group), Wesleyan
  Poetry Series, 2016.
Neptune Park, Omnidawn Publishing, 2013.
Privado, Action Books, 2010.
The Dandelion Clock, Tinfish Press, 2010.
Puppet Wardrobe, Parlor Press, 2006.

Chapbooks

Lost Privilege Company (under the signature of Blunt Research Group),
  Noemi Press, 2016.
Brick Radio, Oystercatcher Press (Norfolk, UK), 2014.

Theory & Criticism

My Silver Planet: A Secret History of Poetry and Kitsch, Johns Hopkins
  University Press, 2014.
In the Poisonous Candy Factory, Capsule Editions (London, UK), 2013.
Infidel Poetics: Riddles, Nightlife, Substance, University of Chicago
  Press, 2009.
Toy Medium: Materialism and Modern Lyric, University of California
  Press, 2000.
Radio Corpse: Imagism and the Cryptaesthetic of Ezra Pound, Harvard
  University Press, 1995.

CRY BABY MYSTIC

Daniel Tiffany

Parlor Press
Anderson, South Carolina
www.parlorpress.com

Parlor Press LLC, Anderson, South Carolina, 29621
© 2021 by Parlor Press
All rights reserved.
Printed in the United States of America
S A N: 2 5 4 - 8 8 7 9

Library of Congress Cataloging-in-Publication Data

Names: Tiffany, Daniel, author. | Thompson, Jon, editor.
Title: Cry baby mystic / Daniel Tiffany ; edited by Jon Thompson.
Description: Free Verse Editions. | Anderson, South Carolina : Parlor
    Press, [2021] | Series: Free verse editions
Identifiers: LCCN 2020046429 (print) | LCCN 2020046430 (ebook) | ISBN
    9781643172026 (paperback) | ISBN 9781643172033 (pdf) | ISBN
    9781643172040 (epub)
Subjects: LCGFT: Poetry.
Classification: LCC PS3570.I335 C79 2021 (print) | LCC PS3570.I335
    (ebook) | DDC 811/.54--dc23
LC record available at https://lccn.loc.gov/2020046429
LC ebook record available at https://lccn.loc.gov/2020046430

978-1-64317-202-6 (paperback)
978-1-64317-203-3 (pdf)
978-1-64317-204-0 (ePub)

2 3 4 5

Cover design by Stephen Scheffler Graphix

Parlor Press, LLC is an independent publisher of scholarly and trade titles in
print and multimedia formats. This book is available in paperback and ebook
formats from Parlor Press on the World Wide Web at http://www.parlorpress.com
or through online and brick-and-mortar bookstores. For submission information
or to find out about Parlor Press publications, write to Parlor Press, 3015
Brackenberry Drive, Anderson, South Carolina, 29621; editor@parlorpress.com.

Contents

Acknowledgments

Thanks to the editors of the following journals, where sections of this poem have been published (in earlier drafts):

Bennington Review
BOMB
Brooklyn Rail
Colorado Review
Denver Quarterly
FENCE
Flash Cove (Australia)
Iowa Review
Journal of Poetics Research (Australia)
New American Writing
The Tiny
Tupelo Quarterly
VOLT
West Branch

Cry Baby Mystic

The creature stood still and would not answer.

Her cryings came but seldom; one bout a month at first, then once a week, afterwards daily. Once she had fourteen.

Her crying was so long and loud it stopped people in their tracks, unless they knew the reasons for her crying.

—The Book of Margery Kempe

Cry Baby Mystic

We know
just when to stop.
They deliver a mess,
we go by the book, whoever
it is.

Ear pitched
to the ocean
floor, clouds of furious
green, one creature held out against
our tricks.

Moon can't
choose where it goes.
A spoon will do. Plucking
down signals she turned to eyeless
stone as

if her
crying bouts could
not yet be annexed to
listen her way in with her mouth.
Not yet.

Dead leaves
and dirty stars.
The door's unlocked, she'll slow
things down and gnaw your backbone half
in two.

Beggar-
bold honey swat
—god this place is freezing—
bareback telepath not just her
own thoughts

a horse
shows up half dead
with a hood pulled over
its head dreaming of what it's like
to live

unseen.
I'm sure it won't
be bribed with sugar cubes.
*Use cold water, it's faster, drain
the head.*

Traffic
spins backward through
the glass redoubt—could that
be why scratchy names make a blue
moon bleed?

I know
you don't just leave
a walnut sitting there.
No one would dare leave a walnut
behind.

That shack
where the road ends
weren't nothing she know'd of,
red and dark red and dark. Nope, not
in here

you don't.
Fool back out of
the smoke hold a candle
to your chin. Gorgon City. On
Margaret's

orders,
my Cavendish:
La doorbell est fuckée.
I won't be sad in this world just
listen.

As if
names could sound like
hammers when the sky blows
into your mouth. How big things seem
seen through

a key-
hole. Whoever
is spying barricades
herself, like the thing spied upon.
Things we

don't know
how to think, we
see! No law down here. Both
out of reach, surprising shyness
could be

a bit
like a first night's
sleep after someone's been
buried, as if daybreak might find
the odd

house ringed
by horses. At
those bleak altitudes how
much less on those who are saved, how
much less.

And as
it happens, said
creature--of whom this book
is written—was present there, too,
giving

the chairs
and tables goose
bumps (popularity
is the bottom 20%
of words

in her
private language
mirror means shovel—not
"jonesing" a euphemism for
the day-

to-day
experience
of being pursued by
objects having nothing to do
with one's

life. Same
deal. Same stall she
took her pregnancy test
in. *Same*. Trust like a spider's web,
Goya's

flashbulb.
I don't know you.
Ark of the mouth-sized bite.
Miss Humpty-Dumpty appears
to be

confused.
One two / bird flew
she leans against the fire
escape, the local fence churning
tugboat

scuttle
in the amen-
corner lockdown, God all
over the floor. It is the dregs
birds crave.

Secrets
don't get away
when you tell them. Jewelry
does a job like that, tormenting
people.

Take me
for thy wyf and
lerne to sing, firstfruits and
the trespass offering, the gift
of the

shoulders.
On the quay ships
sleep as ships alone can
sleep—the bashful ticking struggle
between

you and
yourself. In some
years no sightings at all.
The copy must be signed across
the face.

Candles, oaths and funny hats. Miss Fischer hummed a tune to get things going. You could hear the kids put their friend's name into the usual ring game, but without saying it aloud. It's not easy to make someone who's sitting in the same room with you disappear. Face covered, the child listened until it was time for sentencing to begin—after hearing bits of testimony about shoes and sleepovers. New methods. One or two classmates shed a few tears. It was very sad, a beautiful day, all in all.

A squashed
blackberry stuck
to the sole of my shoe
in Paradise you'll starve up on
the roof.

Mobbing
birds will sometimes
swerve away before they
strike even the motion of hands
to shield

the head
draws more birds so
the targets couldn't be seen
or photographed. I'm not sure how
it works.

[EPILOGUE]

Puddles
sometimes glow but
not for long. A kiss lights
up around your mouth when you die.
Some say

don't go
around counting
people. Why not? They can't
tell. Same with the necklace business,
a face

pissed in
the snow. No one
could have guessed that I'd be
dragging myself like a trunk through
the fields.

Instead
it just happened.
I tiptoed past the guard
fearing I understood only
half of

what I'd
promised to do.
(I'm riding home skyhooked
on a white pig and someone says,
Turn back.

But then
I'll die, I say.
So I turn back, waiting
by myself for them to cut up
the rest.

And then
what? Day gets pulled
cock-eyed into the ground
somewhere between the palm and her
nipple.

I live
in love-longing.
Along came a shelling
girl, she put me in her pail, just
me and

the sand
dollars, LA,
the night cream capital
of the world. Even cops here use
the stuff.

Scarcely
had we arrived
when the years of auto-
hypnosis caught up with us—wait,
we for-

got how
to sleep! It is
the adorable one
who does all the slapping. Her slap-
object

can take
hard slaps without
the slightest discomfort:
prompt, prepared, professional—*fwap!*—
down he

goes a
pale chanting top
two ground-rollers and at
least one honeyguide. A noisy
miner.

The masked
type is not well
known for sibling murder.
Bee-eaters ride secretary
birds side-

saddle.
Full wo thee warp
Huck honey a awful
fix. Aha, one last thing to see
about.

You mean
Natalie Wood?
—who grabbed a knife and used
it as a mirror to check her
lipstick

at a
fancy dinner
party with Bob prowling
around all night in that roadster
of his.

Yes, but the security detail is still in place. Nothing can see you. I promised
to be only what she would want me to be. I insisted that I had become
very reasonable, but she quickly changed the subject!

The lies
themselves began
to take me at my word.
Cord wrapped around a broken pump
letting

itself
be examined
mercilessly—who says
palaces ever were neat and
clean, what

with all
my friends here: *Eye
Winker, Penny Wipe, Lick
Pan, Nose Smeller, Mouth Eater, Chin
Chopper.*

Bones may
be dropped from great
heights to break them open
on the slopes of *Mount Quarentyne.*
Seeing,

thinking,
sobbing's the best
life on earth—watch, he'll knock
on my door when he gets off work
tonight.

Not that
the world's so lost
we need to start packing
our bags. His "divine monstress" he
called me

from his
rotten English:
I savede him from beyting
and he hath me bette. A kissing
ther was.

Pretty
grimy—we're done
with art—you never know
how much inside you is breaking
apart,

what it
must be like, why
some words get their way, some
don't, he spends the night wherever
he lands

We'd still
need to give up
the nest in our skulls, swing
wide of the Earth. Mouth wants to be
alone.

I look
at the trees, they
may not be drunk. The nut
vendor is not the cop but he
could be.

*You must keep your wish to make your wish come true. You must keep
your wishes and keep your wishes. You must keep your wish.*

Out one
day I hear um-
teen ringtones going off
at once—*is that me?*—as the nymphs
ask why

must we
wait for nightfall.
Ful feyne, I clyppe, I kiss.
Just please don't just use him any
old way.

Surely
there is an end.
And our expectations
will not be put off. Much squatting
beside

the key-
hole, unawares.
Tipping up (up ending)
the project, pseudo-epic is
epic.

Delayed
letter, rubber
tubing, winter can't help
it, dingbat. Pucker up, fat doom,
Dingheit.

[CAPTION 1]

And yet
we bar the fleur.
The walk went for a walk,
the wounded room stopped making sounds
today.

Voiceless
tenths of increase,
I want to get her told
—one goes south at eight, one goes north
at nine.

*And there are always gaps. A small, drab, difficult-to-identify bird is often
referred to as a Little Brown Job.*

Who wears
the ears around
here? Miss Bit Middle Mess,
out all night, the one kicking in
my stall.

Thank you.
No one told me
about pagan psycho-
analysis. *Moot* flips to *fil hir
sorwe*.

Girl is
got into her
altitudes, a twig that's
possessed. She tricked Hitler into
a snow-

storm. Don't
ask me how. Wait
a sec. Could that be her?
She knits up her cold but kissy
shoulders:

"Either
of you boys want
a Coke?" I hear a smile
impaled on the coat rack God this
place could

set you
back. Eyes glued to
the breach, yeah, everything's
locked on everything else. There goes
my chance.

Now will
the has-beens lick
my side of the moon, dust
off my ass. I blame myself. *Ain't
no use.*

She played
a gas station
attendant whose gaudy
eye deceived me into destruction.
That thing

between
us? Fresh orphan
junk. Okay, okay, there's
someone crying wolf—I buried
half and

wiped my
tracks. Angelic
something, she said, a brace
of impeccables, soberized,
vap'rish.

[STET]

Ate cake
feels great going
to pieces man yells: *truth
never made sense to me*. No one saw
the day

coming
when she'd grab him
by those massive braids of
his, pull down the canopy
and cut

away
the handsome head.
She tumbles his body
from the bed and stows her trophy,
her bag

of meat.
People screaming
in Tennessee can't get
enough of her "nameless furlough"
trucker

mojo.
No accident
is this. We topped our parts,
all the monosyllables of
surprise.

Bird Brain.
Lonely kettle
de-listing joy, prattle
plague, glance-harm. Digger-truck-spyhole.
Go now.

So the
young man did as
the angel commanded:
You gonna wop that steel on down.
Little

bell call
you, big bell warn
you—answer the door—if
you don't want bad dreams to put mouth
and fore-

head as
far apart as
a face can be. And no
damn door. What do you say to that?
He'll get

the door,
then I'll get it.
No louder than a branch
cracking. I'd hammer my fool self
to death

and pipe
in a quibble
(senselessness kicked over
"the wig scene" back in the day is
my guess

[ALLEGORY 1]

You'll get
your dress dirty
down here. And you won't be
able to stop crying when it starts.
The strange

sounds made
by birds detained
in airless burrows re-
call the noises shoemakers make
working

alone
in their clutter.
The sun is up, a man's
heart can be cured with the ash of
perfume.

But I
knew not the free
sparrows in the wall, how
something ill might one day swallow
their joy,

something
heard, the young plum
trees here so thick you can
hardly make out the abandoned
village

nestled
in their shady
branches. Nor could I use
the simplest phrase, or bring myself
to name

a glass
of milk—more failed
words doing whatever
they want with me. Yet another
useless

word is
EXPERIENCE,
ghost squatting in the mire,
what to say when gulping moonshine,
my shoes

muddied
up by the mash
of dew and dust. *This ain't*
no place to collar no nod—here,
just take

what's left.
She shakes her head,
ticked off, quick blade barely
missing the skin. Because the sewn-
on child

stops her
pain, I knew not
Pluto sunk in greenish
gloom, all caterpillar-colored
because

of the
sins of the world.
Perverse nature, it's true,
loves not that little reptile word
obey.

Surely
my fingers they're
mine but someone else seems
to be using them. Count to ten
and it'll

all be
over. Maybe
those aren't her eyes—maybe
it's just her mouth that looks so wet
from here.

(Such were
the oaths and tears
and sweet conversation
this creature found at the lip of
our grave.

And here follows a very notable instance of the creature's feeling. It is
written down here for convenience, inasmuch as it is, in feeling, like the
matters that have been written before, notwithstanding that it happened
long after the matters that follow.

Through her
skin you could see
a road beating a path
to my door through the cricket smoke.
Now that

she's gone
she lifts her hands,
hollering "Please don't let
'em hurt my boy!" But she's got no
shoes on,

I see.
Is that a fence
there chuckling to itself?
Is that a wig stopping the drain?
The door-

bell is
fucked. *I hate to
see the revelers go,* she
says, the same one whose fingers combed
my hair.

And I
never did pick
more white daisies, not for
fear of her return but because
I was

afraid
of white daisies.
Before long, with a good
pinch, she'd sealed off the cure, her head
bridled

maybe
she got to be
that way in the kitchen
the way kitchens are. If something
goes wrong,

words come
out of nowhere,
there's no turning back, birds
flap like mad at scarecrows of bone
buttons

sewn to
her coat. No one
could tell if she's eating or
just watching, mercifully pale on
the out-

side and
dark blue on the
inside, wearing no crown
astride the moon. I don't get it.
Bughouse

chess, be
my guest. *What I
want you to do now is
take this fine pillow from under
my head.*

I thought
I had the bed
to myself, but someone
grabbed me under the sheets and said
"Do you

recall
the day I caught
you standing in the woods?
I knew you when you didn't know
yourself."

(Whether
they were absent
or present, or klepto-
parasitic, someone set them
on fire.

She found
him and numbered
him and poured him out, un-
vitriol'd skylark and hoax in
common.

Some call
it an egg tooth,
same spurious prologue,
breath-lobe made of gauze and twine and
snowflakes.

Still, this
manner of plain
speaking went on for eight
and a half years during the breach.
Fuck me.

Never
mind what it's called.
It sleeps under a bridge,
it burns through stuff, cracking down it
can't be

found, apt
to pinch the odd
ruderal plant it rhymes
with Creole for *knob*, her left eye
shimm'ring.

*As when a bird has flown through the air, there is no token of its way to
be found, but the light air being beaten with the stroke of its wings, and
parted with the violent noise of them, is passed through, and afterwards
no sign where it went is to be found. Or as when an arrow is shot at
a mark, it parts the air, which quickly comes together again, so that it
cannot be known where it went through.*

I took
off my hat as
I walked to see if the
lace were not scorched, thinking it had
brushed down

a star.
Flames compared to
numbers. *So intricket!*
(Almost gave myself half a lump
trying,

I watched
a guy lose ten
grand crying through the lock.
I brushed the ants aside. *That fetch
won't get*

you in
—a phrase that would
one day make perfect sense.
I tried to sleep it off. My eyes
clattered

open—
someone
was trying to swim up-
river that night. Reason I was
mad was

I knew
right up until
the end. No one's going
to turn into a horse around
here. Throat

seized up,
three times I knocked
at the door. What could she
be laughing about? That greenish
tinge pre-

figured
her extraction
from the world, not mine. Souls,
if not volunteers, strangle each
other

at birth.
(I would wax the
inside too it's even
more scorched. They say you're not supposed
to lift

a curse.
A child will smack
your face and all the birds
sing bass. Old Business. The flowers
growing

dizzy
from being breathed
in. So much shyness. When
it blusters it would rather break
its own

rib than
crack a branch to
house the creche and the flood-
lit toys. Say *yes* and you'll wish you
hadn't.

[CAPTION 2]

Knowledge
of the entire
room sleeps in the mirror:
fish being the fish's lone thought
pattern,

the bread
box is sparkling
too much, the chair must be
the one daydreaming not me. *Wel*
owe I

to weep,
if I of love
can, if I of love can,
my purs al to torn, if I of
love can

And while
he was clearing
out the place I asked him
about proper-name-hatred and void-
stepping.

I went
to the hatters
to buy him a hat but
when I came back he was feeding
the cat.

I went
to the barbers
to buy him a wig but
when I came back he was dancing
a jig.

Only,
sir, one finger
of your right hand, if you
happen to notice, looks somewhat
murky.

His question turned into a long walk from the terrace covered with thick trees. We found only a kind of experienced joke. Secrets, too, attracted me when I was doing my turn. We were long forgotten since we walked. First, he had my arms tied up during my lifting, then that arm somehow or other entwined itself around me, while mine bore him up and prevented him, almost, from touching the ground.

Though some
prefer the old
joints where you strip bareass
in the balcony and slouch down
trap-door

style, steel
toe to Bambi's
spotted coat and the broke-
down chair as more troops crawl up
the dim

steps on
all fours. One poor
soul found nature dismal
with "Steve McQueen" no longer
for rent.

Holding
three lbs. of new
potatoes, thinking about
the irreversibility
of things.

I once
have known a man
soft as death could not catch
my scent no telling where "Little
Hat" went.

Whether
or not I shared
in the spoils I ended
up watching. That was seven years
ago.

[BRACKETS]

They've lost
none of their charm.
The novice detective's
a total stranger, his question
is not

germane
to the murder.
It should be clear by now
what he has hanging between his
legs, a

good piece
of eating stuff
("seafood" as Navy meat
of this grade is called). Have you not
eyes for

the re-
cently erased?
Approaching truth as if
it were a strange dog I try to
recall

how to
use my upscale
sentences. God makes raw
the devil cooks, three stars if you
hit the

stupid
wonderful. And
the hilltop will stand mute
forgetting it spent the night as
a part

of speech.
There is danger,
to be sure, said one nymph
to another. I'm going to eat
your ass

from here
to kingdom come,
brandishing teacups and
worn out phrases. (Her cryings
came but

seldom,
one bout a month
at first, then once a week,
afterwards daily. Once she had
fourteen.

And her
red-eyed captain
won't knock off at night. That
napkin may be the one person
looking

after
her! With a hint
of menace she dips it
in her glass: *Here, sir*, offering
the wet

spot to
him, *your mouth, sir*,
says she. Threats cannot move
her. The stars look as if they can't
stand each

other
yet want to suck
each other off. They've got
that nasty rotten quality
people

pay good
money for, al-
most a mondegreen of
"bitch, I see you" and nonstop wish-
bone talk.

So, yeah,
the gathering crowd
tramples on its faith—some
stand on stools to gape, a people
I know

only
from books, their strange
children will fail and be
afraid out of their prisons and
succumb.

Every
morning they wind
their funnels open / shut
until finally they overwind
them right

into
October. As
they prosper they become
monosyllabic, like forest
rangers,

putting
on that look, that
wholesome obscenity
of theirs—yeah, they're creeps, real pieces
of eating

stuff in
their prime. But hey,
don't worry, we won't make
you do anything weird. And we
have some

new meds
to keep it safe:
blood-boilers. I gave him
a taste, just a wee little dab.
"Why, sir,

it's your
eye that worries
me—it's big as a door!"
(Now don't start that again—people
can tell

when you're
up to no good
so he hands me a list
of Latin secrets from the Burn
Unit

and says
you can't be yelled
at by a tree—under
it, yes, but that's not the tree's fault.
Oh, peek-

a-boo
heart uselessly
trading things, moldy clothes
for seven planks. Reason I'm still
shy of

objects
is simple, I
like them. Old tools and such.
Come on in here where we can get
it good.

[EPILOGUE]

At neck
height the trench digs
itself out. Hair and nails
go nuts in the dark. Come summer-
time rot

chews through
your pelt. I eat
and eat, but my sleep stays
thin. The first bite hurts, the flesh so
cold it

uncoils
into my brains
before I can swallow
it. (Go on, tell them what your *real*
name is.

She don't
even know her
own kind a rat falls out—
that's her head? Like angry words from
a dark

place. Wigs
and rats will get
you killed. No help, can't tell
thinking from doing snap willow
cry switch.

Sorry.
I didn't know
animals are religious.
What can I do to make it up
to you?

Since no
one lives there she
thought to herself why not
say hi to my monster he spits
the gum

out of
his mouth just a
head stuck on a body
I have a rule against blue eyes
but still

she can't
find him. Too bad.
He dropped his Game Boy like
lamp cords don't just drop from the sky
when he

hears the
cornfield rattling
in his forehead! True, this
conversation went on, but how
far on.

A man
fumbling his cap
never quite finds his head.
A knock at the door is almost
the same

as him
hearing music,
you know, things siphoned up
through fourteen layers of je ne
sais quoi.

*The darkness was so wonderful that we could distinguish objects. A girl
who never eats quince like that, a girl who belongs. And through the
transparent wheels of the summer night our imagination was an island in
front of the lodge. The river swarmed with cupids—though we never won
the opposite side.*

Are these
the abandoned
people in the house by
which the ensnared volatile
has been

brought to
bear on its fixed
position a mile and
a half beyond parole? Jinxed have
I not

reason
to sniff the moon
with my probiscus, her
head adorned with seaweed and half
wings of

cockle
shells, a pair of
Piranesian by-
standers "the street" swallows up and
forgets

where it's
going. Either
that or Giant Robot.
Tastee Goodee Chinese open
all night.

Not a
quarter dressed, we
skipped the public toyings
where we might have been modesty'd
by less

tawdry
practicings for
survival of the free-
basing clown in flames. Politeness
will not

live in
a storm. She says
scientists have found sets
from an old movie on the beach.
Farewell

to my
chimerical
system but for the sea
change at the last minute and three
wild notes

on her
housings! Hence the
conceit of my nostrum-
mongership. Really? *You're not her?*
No search

party,
beginner's luck
becoming a deathtrap,
besides, she didn't even use both
hands (my

tempest
tells me so. Off
comes the perfume bottle
stopper, the scent is sharp as dust, like
Cool Whip

thinking:
felicitate
thyself then upon thy
defects! Namely, runaway murked
up *lordz*.

"You have
despised yourself
therefore will you not be
despised by God: night climbs in first,
all sides

at once
faces blown out
chalk to blush and they stay
that way. But he's not home if you
could call

it home.
Lawn the mow, my
bad, the bell that never
rings. You could say he's just around
the bend,

heck, with
mobb deep dropping
hints—*doozy-do*—it gets
sprung on the asphalt like a bare-
foot shoe.

How's that?
They think the things
they see submit to things
they see not. And with the Old Soul
taken

down they
start to whistle
a different tune, you know?
The *down-pressers* come to the door
the sky

itself
rustling and, of
course, we know it never
happens that way. In reality
the blue

tractor's
speed is at least
six times greater than that
of the red tractor. Neither one
reaches

the scene
unfolding in
our heads before they shut
the gates. Play that thing to death. I mean
hello.

Maybe
it all collects
in your hair. I'm not sure
these cops understand it's not like
it was.

You can
ride ride ride through
the night, through the next day
and night, and not hear the bell blow,
if bells

could blow.
Whatever he
heard he heard the man cut
down right there, arm's length, roaring—no,
roaling—

if that's
possible. I
became my own thief, words
knew just how far I'd gone. Kindness
put on

more and
more jewelry till
it froze to death, until
the song became as homesick as
we were.

[ALLEGORY 2]

My sun-
dress looks as if
I'll have to say good bye
for now. Footsteps all I hear, long
chain, name

by for-
gotten name. I
do like guys on the strict
side. My ex-boyfriend hustled me
a job

down in
the slag room: *Jak*
bad me the mouth / thought I
on no gile / better is that ich
oone deye /

thought I
on no gile / turned
wayside word / that's how it
ends. The snow betrayed me, I can't
abide

the cold.
The snow denounced
me. And that's when I heard
barking, baying, as the peaks stared
down through

my head,
dogs blinking wet
like stars. Hoodwink Alley,
mend the fire, who cannot weep come
learn at

me, less
the Heath Hen last
seen the evening of March
11, 1930, at
Martha's

Vineyard,
Massachusetts.
A person climbs out and
never comes home. She said you'd know
the way,

the way.
Her crying went
on forever, it stopped
people in their tracks unless they
knew some

reason
for her crying
When this creature came to
her senses again, a bed of
finger-

hungry
foxgloves played just
the first few bars of *Peter
and the Wolf*. The sky fell over
the grass.

*For similar reasons, the Wryneck has cryptic plumage, probably an
adaptation to the dim light of the forest floor.*

At least
I think that's what
I heard her say: "Let me
in"—or was it, "Let me out"? A
ransacked

night will
do that. Why not
kill the deal now? Inside
a crowded ghost ship, you might hear
sobbing

as dread-
ful in a row
boat. Nice people spit on
friends in horror of their illness.
(My breath

teeters
inside my chest—
bunker, burka, sinkhole.
I'm not a horse, you're not a mil-
lipede

therefore
I need someone
to help me crawl out of
my skin nobody does so I
just wolf

something
down unable
to gauge how the color
black will be doled out. Yonder
comes my

jailer,
broken Danny
Three-Sticks: I understand
what he says to me in English,
and he

follows
what I say, but
I do not comprehend
the English that other people
mutter.

And what
if someone else
echoes him word for word?
It still makes no sense unless he's
the one

talking:
"Will you then do
as I order you to
do?" Very willingly, sir, for
I am

in you
and you are in
me. From this sign you may
know that I have endured many
sharp words.

Soon he
will not be fit
to choose, his throat become
an open sepulcher: *Desire*
of me

and I
shall give thee the
heathen for thine utmost
inheritance. (Hmm, better not
google

that scene
—what are those horse
veins on my neck?—as if
dying weren't always in someone
else's

house, each
of us given
a mouth with a roof—wake
not too roughly, he needs a code
word for

what he
does to me. Turns
out he's expert in holes
& hinterlands, my share, messed-up
object

hurled from
afar, the in-
direct world taking shape
before my very eyes. Best lay
low now, sweet

faether
deed faether deed
faether deed faether deed
faether deed faether. I believe
I'll dust

[TABLE]

my broom.
Streams run dry, stones
are placed. One such "hunger
stone" reads: *Neither visited nor
visiting.*

To speak
in clouds and run
away from the subject—
who is not of the same flesh he
deceives?

Fur stinks
when it burns. Go
ahead, build the fire! Ab-
sence from the nest—"nest neglect"—dopes
the preen

gland of
the clerk. On that
day in the chapterhouse
there were many people waiting
to see

what would
be said and done
to break said creature: "You,
wolf, what is that cloth you have on?"
Here she

excerpts
*The Wonder Book
of the Spoilt Earth*: "Sir, it
is wool." A low sound went up from
the crowd.

(Today
it was a ship
on the high seas or, if
not the corn growing, a trinket
playing

the flute.
*The creature stood
still and would not answer.*
Who cannot recall what a peach
looks like?

Not even
homesickness could
track down her scent. And now
to find the flowered suit does not
tarnish!

We all
once looked roughly
alike. Yellow-gold, with
delicate fuzz, and a little
red silk

around
the pit. But I
won't tell you what I am.
Step by step I follow my feet
unsure

whose tracks
these are. *Why art*
thou so far from helping
me and from these whispered words? Friends,
take me

away
from here. I'm no
heretic, the stain rinsed
out crops up again, like old rags
smoldering

without
flame for who knows
how long, an afternoon,
even until the stars come out,
if they

still do.
I wouldn't know.
I'm not sure what she is
supposed to do with me. For one
beer and

one scotch
I might, and for
the surfeit of her lone-
some task, burn right through what's left
of me

—she got
that sweater off
a dead person—and put
said creature to the test, sometimes
lasting

thirty
hours, sometimes
twenty, sometimes ten—it
depends—sometimes more if she tries,
sometimes

two, so
hard and so sharp.
She makes me fight for it.
No surprise there. A cuff link can't
walk, I

can't just
call out HEY GUARD.
My leg must be broken.
We seem to be riding a train
through some

endless
storm. When she smiles
it's a trap, there's nowhere
to turn and none here by that name
but she

knows mine
and I must get
away before she speaks
it aloud. She spins to reach past
the bare

threadwings
of the dragon-
fly, to grasp its body
firmly and to keep its wings, once
it tears

off its
own barbed eye, free
from the bird's face as it
smacks its prey against a perch. And
yes, I

enjoy
these horrible
sights. The smell of invaded
countryside. We're the only ones left
around

here. We
obey ourselves.
Melodramatic junk.
And there's always the chance she'll get
something

wrong, may-
be everything.
By taking things last night
to make her sick if nothing else
would do.

[STET]

Why do
you insist? There's
nothing here. The timer's
broken, lightbulbs flare, jaw soldiers
and gland

soldiers
work round-the-clock.
The moratorium
on speaking her name must be kept
up. *Please*

take me
away from here.
Night-frost sugared the mess
some kind soul now prods with a rake
—easy

does it—
no one knows what
to do, of course. We cry
out. The parking lot's standing on
its head.

Nothing
ensures the jinx
will ever be dislodged.
People can't help fixing to gob
on life

—suspect—
teeth showing breath-
bellows at full extent
pink froth on whiskers. I'm not quite
done yet,

teacher.
She takes my name
becoming one of us
to jack off the referendum.
Help out!

We shoo
away the songs,
they crawl back into us,
staring off into space where no
one moves.

Ask that
bird if it's ok.
Suddenly you pull down
the branches and eat. But the good
word won't

have time
to climb inside
your head before you say
it aloud. It will mix itself what-
ever

way it
wants. I am no
machine I must stay out
of all the mixes and make sure
no one

knows why,
a sentence dropped
off behind someone's face.
And don't be looking at me like
that! Old

Standards
bent and blazed for
fear of the quota soon
to be hushed by a glimpse of things
to come:

there, she's
hunched inside me
holding a knife—if that's
the right word—no longer living
but not

quite dead
either. I wish
to make a last-minute
request to bracket said creature,
who moans

slumped in
the push-push chair,
eaten away by people's
talk. (Think of the *push-push*, Margie
—no rules—

and give
me instruction.
Please, friends, take me away
from here. I can't go on talking
about

the ones
who wind up face-
down in a ditch somewhere.
Rude songs shall be heard in accord
with her

wish not
to be found. We'll
take the roundabout way.
Hence at the animal crossing
we tip

a cap
of expectation
to all creatures, a cap
for better times. Legend has it
they will

return
on March 19
the resplendent Quetzal
the Chinstrap Penguin colony
the Horned

Screamer
and the Motmot,
all Passeriformes, all
Curlews, the occasional vagrant,
Nightjars

and Loons
and Goatsuckers.
Nobody wants me now
but I am not allowed to leave.
How did

you get
here, they ask. Birds
and birds alone, though some
might not agree, have feathers and
that may

be one
way to explain
a melody I heard
one day, a song so simple and
pure it

just won't
quit. *The chair starts
to smolder*. I'm one of
the people who say that. I don't
know where

I am
supposed to sleep.
And I resolved never
again to approve her feelings
except

they are
mine, too. Many
here who once feigned friendship
to her now hang back out of dread,
little

vain dread
stirred by the sound
of these words, these stanzas
shoved aside, *Les Inferno*, mud
oboe.

They make
her sit at one
end of the table be-
low all others so she dares not
speak and

before
long said creature
placed at the end of said
table speaking not a word lifts
her spoon.

(Looking
out the window
toward the gas fields I see
a burning well. *Cuckoo Clock*, she
calls him,

*my slum-
lord*, and hands me
a list. I pass it to
her Keeper. That's impossible,
he says.

Balling
her hand into
a fist she extends her
finger over the edge, staring
at me

for like
three whole minutes
before declaring "cats
are not dogs" and I believe her.
You could

hear her
name boycotting
every thistle leaf, like
a plate falling off a table.
But she

has some-
thing else in mind.
"Already?" I ask of some-
one who likes to twist you-know-what.
Halting

birdcalls
shoot from the trees.
Her eyes fill entire worlds.
The world is in itself. As if
things had

gone back
to the way they
were before the wool got
burnt by the frost. What does it smell
like? It

smells like
secret police.
A stitch comes loose, a piece
of the bird necklace breaks away.
Could corn

growing
in a field be
her most secluded thought?
Someone runs off into the dark
after

being
asked for help. Who
knows how long she's been gone.
A false mouth opens on the arm.
She too

looks not
to be hurt, her
ersatz-brother moaning
proof she would not be saved from what
she hears.

About the Author

Daniel Tiffany is a poet and theorist who divides his time between Los Angeles and Berlin. He is the author of five previous full-length collections of poetry, including *Privado* (Action Books, 2010), *The Dandelion Clock* (Tinfish, 2010), and *Neptune Park* (Omnidawn, 2013), along with chapbooks from Oystercatcher Press and Noemi. Poems and documentary sources from his collection, *The Work-Shy* (Wesleyan University Press, 2016), published under the signature of BLUNT RESEARCH GROUP, have been adapted for theater and incorporated into museum exhibitions across the U.S. Tiffany's poetry has appeared in journals such as Paris Review, Poetry, Tin House, jubilat, Lana Turner, Fence, Iowa Review, Volt, Poetry Project Newsletter, Bomb, Chicago Review, Brooklyn Rail, and many others. In addition, five volumes of his literary criticism have been published by presses including Harvard and Johns Hopkins, as well as the University of Chicago and the University of California. He is the author of the entry on "Lyric Poetry" in the *Oxford Encyclopedia of Literature*. Apart from his own writing, he has published translations from French, Greek, and Italian writers. He is a recipient of the Berlin Prize, awarded by the American Academy in Berlin.

www.danieltiffany.com

Free Verse Editions

Edited by Jon Thompson

13 ways of happily by Emily Carr
& in Open, Marvel by Felicia Zamora
Alias by Eric Pankey
At Your Feet (A Teus Pés) by Ana Cristina César, edited by Katrina
    Dodson, trans. by Brenda Hillman and Helen Hillman
Bari's Love Song by Kang Eun-Gyo, translated by Chung Eun-Gwi
Between the Twilight and the Sky by Jennie Neighbors
Blood Orbits by Ger Killeen
The Bodies by Christopher Sindt
The Book of Isaac by Aidan Semmens
The Calling by Bruce Bond
Canticle of the Night Path by Jennifer Atkinson
Child in the Road by Cindy Savett
Condominium of the Flesh by Valerio Magrelli, trans. by Clarissa Botsford
Contrapuntal by Christopher Kondrich
Country Album by James Capozzi
Cry Baby Mystic by Daniel Tiffany
The Curiosities by Brittany Perham
Current by Lisa Fishman
Day In, Day Out by Simon Smith
Dear Reader by Bruce Bond
Dismantling the Angel by Eric Pankey
Divination Machine by F. Daniel Rzicznek
Elsewhere, That Small by Monica Berlin
Empire by Tracy Zeman
Erros by Morgan Lucas Schuldt
Fifteen Seconds without Sorrow by Shim Bo-Seon, trans. by Chung Eun-
    Gwi and Brother Anthony of Taizé
The Forever Notes by Ethel Rackin
The Flying House by Dawn-Michelle Baude
Ghost Letters by Baba Badji
Go On by Ethel Rackin
Here City by Rick Snyder
Instances: Selected Poems by Jeongrye Choi, trans. by Brenda Hillman,
    Wayne de Fremery, & Jeongrye Choi
The Magnetic Brackets by Jesús Losada, trans. by M. Smith & L. Ingelmo
Man Praying by Donald Platt

A Map of Faring by Peter Riley

The Miraculous Courageous by Josh Booton

Mirrorforms by Peter Kline

No Shape Bends the River So Long by Monica Berlin & Beth Marzoni

Not into the Blossoms and Not into the Air by Elizabeth Jacobson

Overyellow, by Nicolas Pesquès, translated by Cole Swensen

Parallel Resting Places by Laura Wetherington

Physis by Nicolas Pesquès, translated by Cole Swensen

Pilgrimage Suites by Derek Gromadzki

Pilgrimly by Siobhán Scarry

Poems from above the Hill & Selected Work by Ashur Etwebi, trans. by
    Brenda Hillman & Diallah Haidar

The Prison Poems by Miguel Hernández, trans. by Michael Smith

Puppet Wardrobe by Daniel Tiffany

Quarry by Carolyn Guinzio

remanence by Boyer Rickel

Republic of Song by Kelvin Corcoran

Rumor by Elizabeth Robinson

Settlers by F. Daniel Rzicznek

Signs Following by Ger Killeen

Small Sillion by Joshua McKinney

Split the Crow by Sarah Sousa

Spine by Carolyn Guinzio

Spool by Matthew Cooperman

Summoned by Guillevic, trans. by Monique Chefdor & Stella Harvey

Sunshine Wound by L. S. Klatt

System and Population by Christopher Sindt

These Beautiful Limits by Thomas Lisk

They Who Saw the Deep by Geraldine Monk

The Thinking Eye by Jennifer Atkinson

This History That Just Happened by Hannah Craig

An Unchanging Blue: Selected Poems 1962–1975 by Rolf Dieter Brinkmann,
    trans. by Mark Terrill

Under the Quick by Molly Bendall

Verge by Morgan Lucas Schuldt

The Visible Woman by Allison Funk

The Wash by Adam Clay

We'll See by Georges Godeau, trans. by Kathleen McGookey

What Stillness Illuminated by Yermiyahu Ahron Taub

Winter Journey [Viaggio d'inverno] by Attilio Bertolucci, trans. by
    Nicholas Benson

Wonder Rooms by Allison Funk

www.ingramcontent.com/pod-product-compliance
Lightning Source LLC
Chambersburg PA
CBHW022034090426
42741CB00007B/1062